WELCOME TO THE EARTH SCHOOL

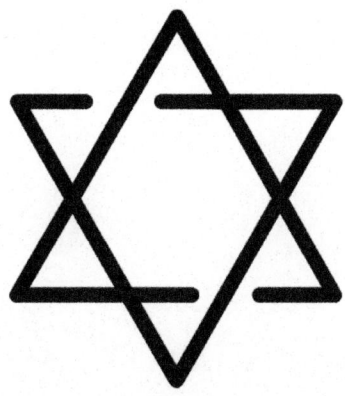

A Wisdom Book On Becoming A Man of Divinity

By: Jesse Sternberg

Dear son,

As you enter manhood, I want you to know that I'm incredibly proud of you.

I know you will become an outstanding man. As your gift for your Bar Mitzvah, I wrote down everything that I know that's of value on the topic of becoming a true man.

This knowledge is valuable at any age.

Introduction

The information in this book will help you in all aspects of your life: money, health, friendships, women, happiness, G-d, etc.

It is not designed to be a book that you read cover to cover at the age of 13 and that's it. Nor is it something that you need to study.

Keep this book safely tucked away, and when you feel the impulse to open it, open it anywhere you like.

Or, simply put, if you're missing me or want to feel my love, open the book.

You can put your hand on the cover and know that my love for you is infinite and eternal and I poured all my wisdom into these pages.

Often what you didn't know you needed, jumps off the page, or floats into your heart.

Your wisdom will come through your own experiences of life. There's no wrong way up the mountain.

Table of Contents

Introduction 3

CHAPTER 1 6

My Spiritual Awakening 6

CHAPTER 2 9

Choices About Life 9

CHAPTER 3 12

Mastering the Human Experience 12

CHAPTER 4 17

On Being a Man 17

CHAPTER 5 22

Women 22

CHAPTER 6 29

Your Mind 29

CHAPTER 7 33

Love 33

CHAPTER 8 35

Medicine, Food and Poison 35

CHAPTER 9 42

Drugs and Addictions 42

CHAPTER 10 47

Money and Material Objects 47

CHAPTER 11 50

Knowledge 50

CHAPTER 12 52

Earth 52

CHAPTER 13 54

G-d 54

CHAPTER 14 56

Law 56

CHAPTER 15 58

The Law of One 58

CHAPTER 16 60

The Law of Karma 60

CHAPTER 17 63

The Law of Attraction 63

CHAPTER 1

My Spiritual Awakening

When I was 27 I had a Kundalini awakening experience.

A lightning bolt of white light rose from the bottom of my spine and crackled its way up to my skull. I turned into white light sound. I heard thunder. I lost track of my body, of time, and I felt a bliss that I've still never felt again, yet I chased after it endlessly.

When I came out of the experience, I was deeply changed.

Profound effects lingered for three days.

My mind had no thoughts.

I was deeply peaceful.

I was kind to everyone.

I was loving towards everything and everyone.

Instead of negative thoughts running rampant in my head, I felt new things, like the wind on my skin. I heard the birds chirping in the background for the first time. I was not only unaffected by the things that used to stress me out, I felt completely at ease.

I didn't know what happened to me, but I knew I needed to make that happen again.

Nothing compared to that experience.

Actually, nothing still has, which is why I have pursued spirituality with such passion.

Along my spiritual journey I have studied many approaches to human life on earth, experienced many truths about manhood, and I have even met and spoke to God.

Yet these topics of my study are ever expanding, and the more I learn, the more I realize I hardly know anything.

One thing I do know for sure though, is that my love for you is as vast as the Universe.

And now begins the lessons I have learned about life, manhood, earth, G-d, divinity, health, and how to master the human experience.

CHAPTER 2

Choices About Life

It doesn't matter if you don't know what you want to do in your life.

Trust that you will know it when you see it.

In the meantime, stay calm and seek the path of highest fun, joy, or gratitude.

You will attract to you what's perfect for you.

This is true for a job, moving to a new city, finding your loving partner. It's even true for what you should do later in the afternoon.

The trick is to stay in the flow state and let things come to you. Also to catch yourself when you're not, and pivot back in. Easier said than done sometimes. This is a skill worth mastering.

Never do what others want you to do unless you also want to.

Pleasure is a distraction from the senses. When you're deeply in the flow state, you won't be distracted by your senses. Synchronicities will appear and everything that you need to know, need to have, or need to do become obvious.

Those who always choose pleasure become weak and ill. Pleasure is an impulse.

There is nothing left after your pursuit of pleasure and it is often a setback.

For example, eating bad food, seeking a cheap thrill, these have costs on your mental and physical health.

Learn this early and you will thrive.

I have seen in my own life how discipline brings freedom, inner peace, and superior health.

Choose things that nourish your body, your mind and your heart. Your soul will be happy even if the choice feels challenging. Pay attention to how your body and soul feel after your choices.

Choose things that flow to you and make you feel good.

Choose things that are fun to do that do not harm or disrespect others.

Always choose the path of highest joy available to you at any moment. Then do that activity with passion. That is the key to success.

These things are easy to say, but difficult to remember.

Reflect on this last statement often and your life will be masterful.

You will achieve everything you want with minimal effort, maximum energy and a sense of effortlessness.

This is how the masters do it.

CHAPTER 3

Mastering the Human Experience

Mastering the human experience is like having really good emotions, a calm mind, and superior strength and flexibility of the body well beyond what is considered normal.

This trinity (mind, body and emotions) affects one another. Each is connected to the others. Never forsake one for the expansion of another.

Having balance in these three things is a treasure few people have.

Whatever life throws your way, trust that it is good because it forces your soul to grow.

Staying calm and balanced helps the pain of growth subside. Growth is often uncomfortable. That is not a reason to avoid it, because growth is why you are here and it is inevitable. Earth is a school for the soul.

Trust that even if life knocks you down, you have the strength to get back up. Get back up even if you feel weak, for the action of moving forward in life brings you energy.

Even if angry, sad, or hurt, when you get back up, do it swiftly, with grace, with stoicism. This is true strength and it's always inspiring to watch.

Learn how to observe your body breathing itself at all times. That's the easiest way to know you're in the flow.

Train your mind to feel your breath in your chest, your belly, or in the hairs of your nostrils at all times. This is what the Buddha taught his son.

Breath is the King of the mind, the link to your Soul, and your anchor in the present moment, or the flow state. This is what the ancient yogis have always known.

Since nothing exists outside of the eternal present moment, seek to anchor your attention deeply in the moment. Other people, emotions and stories of the mind will seek to pull you into the past or the future.

It's masterful to stay graceful in the moment regardless of what is happening to your mind, body or emotions.

You will find no calmness when your mind is thinking about the past or worrying about the future.

The moment is all you ever have, learn to stay here.

No moment is ever the same.

No river is the same stepping into it twice.

No situation can ever be repeatable.

This is true for all things that will ever happen to you for your entire life.

When it comes to money, or material objects, or feeling safe: it's not about how much you have, it's about how much you Love.

Love and Gratitude attracts everything you desire to you effortlessly.

Never judge others.

God is the judge of all things and he is fair, even if you can't see it yet.

It's worth remembering that you get what you give, just not from whom you gave it to. Do not let this be a reason why you give. Give because it feels good. Give because you know we are all One, and others are in need of what you have in abundance.

Similarly, if you give something bad, disrespectful, distasteful, or accidentally cause harm, this experience will happen back to you. The Universe teaches this way. It's called the Golden rule.

Don't be in a rush to get a job, start a career, become a man, get married or have children. That's simply doing something because you feel you have to. Society will pressure you otherwise.

Indeed, it is the case that when you are following your bliss, all of these things will present themselves to you and you will know in your heart that they are right for you.

Everything that's perfect for you unfolds in divine timing.

Life in a human body on earth is very short compared to the infinity of time.

Yet your soul lives forever.

It's possible to die when you want.

When the time comes, your body will release chemicals taking away pain, so never fear dying. This the primal fear for all humans and it's masterful to transcend it.

In the moments leading up to your death stay with your breath and bring your attention into your third eye.

If you do this, then you can die consciously, blissfully, and remember everything about this life in your next life.

That is truly mastering life.

CHAPTER 4

On Being a Man

As a man evolves, he should strive to become divinely masculine.

Men should strive to develop the personality and skills of a selfless King, the Mage, the Peaceful Warrior, or the Inspiring Poet, for each of these represents the archetype of a man expressing his highest potential as a man.

Few men are aware of this, yet when you embody any of these roles, you are extremely useful, therefore success is imminent.

It is rare to be skillful in all four, yet I encourage you to choose this path.

For you will be as G-d among men. Respected by everyone, wise, wealthy, humble, and of significant service to earth, her humans, and her animals.

You will be able to create anything you desire, stand firm in the face of any fear, change any circumstance at will, create justice for yourself and others, and generate love, peace and compassion for many!

This is the path of the Humble Emperor, strive for it, for you are capable of achieving true greatness.

When a Humble Emperor conquers, those he conquered are happy to align themselves with him!

For he enhances every aspect of their lives. You will become a man other men wish to be around, and a man that women wish to have as their own.

The highest path is to conquer the world and your dreams without destruction, with love, with purity, with innocence and leave no trace of yourself.

The divine is anonymous and mysterious.

Therefore, it's wise to keep a little bit of mystery about yourself in all your relationships.

It makes you fun and interesting.

My observations about most older men is that they are still boys at the emotional level. They cannot control themselves or their impulses.

They seek self-gain like a child would.

They require others to help them as a little boy requires his mother.

Watch for this, for when they are hurt, they unknowingly hurt others.

Therefore, age, money, power, strength without control... accumulating these things does not make you a man.

We are all interconnected, and a true man has the wisdom to realize this at all times.

Once you are strong, wise, and powerful, seek to serve the many. This will give you tremendous joy and doorways will open up for you.

Being selfless with your energy, humble with your power, wise and compassionate, and strong enough to deal with our own pain, this is a true man.

Choose to be of true service to others. Your presence will make them feel safe. Your wisdom will give them strength.

You are capable of doing this now my boy with your friends, your sister and mother, our animals, and your teammates.

This brings me much pride.

Always seek to develop more discipline with regard to strengthening and nourishing your body, your mind, and your ability to stay present in the moment.

Know that as life tests you, you will endure everything. G-d does not give you anything your soul cannot handle.

With these virtues, you will grow naturally into your divinely masculine nature.

Growth is essential for your soul, and doing so allows more of God's energy to come to earth and inhabit your body.

Remember this when you are scared.

Giving in to fear stops the growth, takes your energy, brings discomfort, and if prolonged can make you sick in the mind, body or emotions.

More of God's energy means more power to manifest what you want more speedily.

More healing power to cure genetic deficiencies.

More mental ability, and supernatural powers can blossom.

Don't be a fool and think these do not exist simply because most humans haven't discovered them.

Few men are truly protectors and providers, yet that was our role in ancient times.

Strive to become excellent at both. Practice a martial art and attract wealth. Do this for yourself.

Create your own kingdom doing and enjoying what you love, do not focus on having a queen before you have these.

This is the wisest and most selfless thing you can do, because it allows you to be a better man for those you love.

If you excel at these, you will never have to chase after a woman, for they happen to find this very appealing.

You will attract her by being completely at ease with yourself.

CHAPTER 5

Women

Respect all humans equally, yet realize all souls are not equal.

Some souls are ancient, having lived many lifetimes on earth. You are one of them which is why you are wise. Others, this is their first time here.

Therefore, from G-d's perspective, age and gender should not affect the amount of respect shown to anyone, yet at the same time, it is not true that men and women are equal.

It is foolish to think otherwise. Do not have a sense of pride or ego, believing you are better than any other soul, man or woman, but understand your nature and seek to enhance it.

Know that G-d is genderless. Nature is genderless.

This means their masculine and feminine energies are completely balanced.

Appreciate that each human has a masculine and feminine part.

Your work is to bring your masculine and feminine natures into harmony, but never forget that you are a man.

Men and women have very different natures.

Reflect on this so you can become a better man for the women in your life.

Women are more vulnerable physically.

They have been taken advantage of by men's greed, lust and physicality throughout the ages, and as a collective, they carry trauma because of this.

It is very manly to make women feel emotionally safe in your presence, for this lets them express their true feminine qualities. That is something they wish to be able to do.

Know that the feminine energy is notoriously wiser, more inherently loving and intuitive, and more patient than the masculine energy.

Women are designed to be nurturing when they are in their feminine energy.

When it comes to a romantic relationship, women are repulsed by men who make them feel unsafe.

This feeling of lack of safety throws their feminine-masculine energy out of balance, for now they feel they must protect themselves, which is masculine in nature.

Therefore, if you ever sense a woman is being fearful, aggressive or intimidating, understand she doesn't feel safe and secure.

Seek to make her feel safe and watch her become loving once again.

The virtues of respect, stoicism, emotional control, softness of speech, calmness, these are divinely masculine.

They make others feel wonderful in your presence.

Therefore, master your emotions and your speech.

Strengthen your body.

Discipline your work ethic.

Learn and practice a martial art.

I have already said this, it's worth repeating.

Knowing how to protect yourself will make you feel unconquerable and confident in all situations and highly attractive to women, especially if you remain humble all the while.

Never use anger or aggression towards a woman, it is ungentlemanly. It also reveals a lack of self-control and is manipulative.

While you might be able to make a woman do something she doesn't want to do, this is never a good idea because all humans want to be free.

When you're dating a woman, never let jealousy show, for it will only work against you.

If a woman continues to make you jealous, after you have expressed your feelings, she's not the one.

Find a woman who you can feel totally safe to speak your heart to. You will feel secure and have no jealousy.

Learn to give a woman space.

Absence makes the heart grow fonder. She will miss you and appreciate you even more. Do this naturally by focusing on your own life first.

It's always better to let a woman come to you, than for you to go to her.

Pay note to this. Just as men have used their strength and intimidation to get what they want; women too have a secret weapon that you should know about.

Women are known for using touch, affection, and sweet words to manipulate men who are fond of them for gain, even if they don't truly mean it.

This is not a divinely feminine way of operating, and in this world, this tactic does exist.

I have fallen pretty to this, as have many men without ever knowing. It's where we are most vulnerable and underdeveloped. This tactic works on boys, but it doesn't work on men.

A man knows to trust the actions of people (men and women) over their words.

Actions always reveal a person's true intent.

If the actions and words align, they are trustworthy.

If it does not align, there is no need to call this to attention to a woman. Simply make note, reflect on the action and the word, then act peacefully with your own interests and heart.

A man must always respect himself, and sometimes this looks like making a sacrifice, taking a step backwards, or making a really hard decision so that you have a better future.

Lying to yourself, not noticing what's right in front of you, not noticing that you are being taken advantage of, not valued, not receiving the style of love that you need, or that things are not as they seem, these are common weaknesses for boys.

Another unfortunate truth about our current reality is that Women and children are not really held accountable for their words and emotions.

They can both have outbursts of anger, sadness, stress, and men will not lose any respect for them. A true man will want to help them.

Yet this is not true in reverse.

A man must not lose control of his words or emotions, for when he does, he comes off as scary, unpredictable, and untrusting.

Therefore, if a man is not capable of remaining stoic, a sad truth is that he will lose the respect and the attraction of a woman. He will certainly take her out of her feminine energy.

This may not happen quickly. Rest assured it will happen.

The reason is unconscious. It's because you are no longer perceived as a competent protector or provider.

Therefore, I will remind you again, seek to master yourself in resourcefulness, in physicality, in your emotional intelligence and in your career and let the right woman find you.

CHAPTER 6

Your Mind

Your mind cannot always be trusted.

You are not your mind.

Yet, what you think you become. This is how creation works. This is happening whether you want it to or not. It's always happening.

Always seek to develop your original ideas about how things work.

Seek your own knowledge through your own experience.

The exception to this is if something was written by a master, it's worth trusting even if you don't have any personal experience.

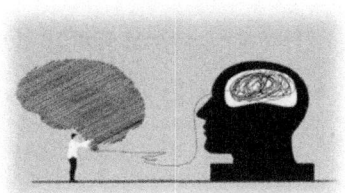

Similarly, the ancient texts can be trusted as well, though they are often encoded.

Aside from thoughts, which are always at the front of your mind, you also have beliefs.

Beliefs are hidden in your unconscious mind. That means you don't really know you have them but you do.

Most of your beliefs are not truly yours.

For example, you inherited them from Zaidy, Bubbie, Amma, Papa, your parents, school, tv, books, the news, the internet, coaches, teachers, etc.

Reflect on that.

Then reflect on who taught them? And why were they taught these!

Now do you see what I mean by most of your beliefs are not truly your own. They just showed up there and the risk is that you go on believing them without questioning them.

Why am I telling you to explore your beliefs?

Because when you understand them, many of your fears in life will vanish. Anxiety will vanish, and what's left over will be peace, wisdom, and tranquility.

Know that the mind can play tricks on you.

This is especially true when you are in a state of fear, anxiety, or uncertainty.

In these states, you cannot always trust the thoughts. Learn to dispose of them using wisdom and discernment.

It's good to use the phrase "how does this thought serve me", and then notice what happens.

It's also effective to notice the feeling and say out loud "I feel scared, sad, or whatever it is, because I believe this is my best choice".

If it is a negative emotion, the energy will ground down and stop persisting because you are closing the thought loop. If the emotion is positive, then it will amplify.

Seek to keep your own mind calm and clear so you can tune into the subtle feelings and thoughts your body sends you.

The body never lies.

These intuitions or sensations will always feel good when you follow their instructions. If a situation feels bad, then leave. If an idea feels good, follow it.

Always listen and do what feels good.

These are messages from G-d's mind.

For G-d's mind is alive and within all and will always be leading you towards discovering your True Nature, the G-d within you!

Develop your intuition, the voice in your head and your gut. This is another name for G-d's mind.

This is all part of exploring and understanding your Self.

Learn to trust your intuition and you will live an extraordinary life.

Never give in to fear because it will block your spiritual growth and distract you from your intuition.

Always trust your first instinct and follow it.

When following your instincts, it's ok to be cautious and dip your toe in the water, to reassess the situation if you're unsure.

Do this over and over and you will live a glorious life.

CHAPTER 7

Love

Love is not what we think it is. It is much bigger than the love of a father or mother.

True Love is how G-d loves, and its power and wisdom is always expanding, just like the Universe.

Strive to understand this and your experience of life will be heavenly.

There are different flavours of love, and they do not come easily to most.

Therefore, study this list and become a master of them all, then you will become a true master on earth.

Standing up for yourself, whether it be justice or righteousness, this is love.

Staying humble, kind, yet flexing your true power, this is courage.

Courage is love.

Forgiving yourself, or those who have wronged you, frees your heart from pain and creates a peaceful future, this is love for your Self.

Being kind and compassionate to ALL, because we are all ONE, this is the love of G-d. Dig for this feeling always.

You don't have to like someone that you love.

You don't have to like someone that hurts you.

Yet choosing to be kind, to restrain your primal desire for revenge or retaliation, this is also self-love, because it removes anger from your heart and gives you peace.

CHAPTER 8

Medicine, Food and Poison

There is a very fine line between medicine and poison.

The line is the dosage, the belief, the intention, the frequency of use, and the reason for using.

Pay attention to these things.

Lots of medicines can be toxic, and many toxic things in small doses can be healing.

Understand the business of medicine.

Pharmacies did not invent medicine.

Pharmacies are corporations, and they prefer that you do not fully heal, for that makes them better at business.

Pharmacies care about creating profit, and they are under pressure to create more profit year over year.

They are the leading profit creators on all the planet and though they have invented beautiful things, they have also caused much harm in their approach.

Pharmacies have never created health that heals humans, for if they did, they would be out of business.

Realize that all medicines created by pharmacies are derivatives of plants. The plants were studied, then made into synthetic medicines that are sold for very high prices. It's a business.

Plants are the original medicine because they were created by G-d. The Rain Forests are where these plants grow, and these forests must be protected for much unexplored knowledge lies within them.

What do you think humans and Shamans used for millennia?

While no medicine can truly heal disease, they will offer you relief from symptoms and pain.

Both plants and pharma are legitimate in that way, and it's wise to use what's affordable, safe and available, for it is not wise to suffer unnecessarily.

Yet, thinking something outside of you can heal you makes you a victim, and this unconscious belief attracts negative experiences to you without your realization.

Doctors cannot heal you. They can perform a surgery. They can prescribe a pill.

But only you can heal you with your thoughts, beliefs, and actions to nourish all parts of you (mind, body, emotions).

Does the tree need medicine?

No, it keeps growing and nature heals it.

We are nature too.

Believing that you need something to heal you is admitting that you can't heal yourself, and this thought creates a blocking from healing naturally.

All illness, all disease, comes from not being at ease in the mind, body or emotions.

This has been known by the sages of old.

That's what dis-ease means.

It means not being at ease!

So, what causes dis-ease?

Negative thoughts.

Negative situations.

Pain in the body that you don't address, that you don't bring love to.

Habits that hurt you without knowing you're doing them.

Negative people around you.

Toxic foods.

Do you see how poison can be many different things?

Therefore, always seek to master your body and express it to the fullest potential so it can tolerate much distress.

Seek to create a strong vessel, using your nutrition, your mind, and proper exercise.

Drink clean water, for your body is mostly fluid.

Avoid foods that can last in the cupboard for long times. They are filled with poisonous preservatives. These do not leave the body very quickly, and lead to discomfort and dis-ease.

Organic fruits and vegetables are medicine.

They create a body that thrives, but this is not enough to develop muscle.

Natural fats and natural proteins will create balance within your body and build a strong physique even if not working out.

Many plants contain fats and proteins, seek to discover them.

Develop a taste for fresh foods. And stay open to eating animals, for all meat contains all essential vitamins and minerals to thrive.

G-d provided animals for us to eat, yet he also asked us to honor them before we eat them.

Therefore, stop eating solely for taste and for pleasure and study the ingredients of what you're actually eating. Is it a list of chemicals or is it real food grown from the earth?

Let food become your medicine. This takes a lifetime to discover, there is no rush. This is part of your mastery.

Learn to listen to your body after you eat.

If you feel tired, the food you ate wasn't good.

If you feel dull, the food you ate wasn't nourishing.

If you feel stable in your energy, peaceful in your thoughts, the food you ate is nourishing.

Avoid sugars over the long run. Though they are fine in moderation, in the long run they accelerate aging.

Do not eat sugary foods within two hours before bed. If you are hungry, eat something with fat and protein. Meat, cheese, beans, soups. Explore these with an open mind and watch what happens to your body.

At night is when the body goes into healing and restoring mode.

Sugar turns that receptor off, slowing your body's ability to heal and build strength.

In short, medicine is an excellent way to bring your body back into balance quickly.

Often when it's in balance, the body itself will stay there. This Is called homeopathy and it's how healers and medicine men have helped humans for eternity.

Therefore, medicine of either pharmaceutical or plant nature is good, in small short doses only if it brings the body back in balance.

Continuous use of these drugs however, is slowly poisoning and creates addiction and anxiety.

Always seek the original source of your discomfort.

Look at your thoughts and emotions as your primal clues.

CHAPTER 9

Drugs and Addictions

Medicine and drugs are closely related.

I am referring now to 'street drugs' or recreational drug usage.

These drugs fall into two categories.

The first is plant medicine, the second is man made medicine.

There are two reasons why people take these.

The first is for fun, or peer pressure.

The second is to cope with their emotional trauma, yet often people don't see this.

If G-d made it, then it's fine to take in small doses.

A small dose of mushrooms, marijuana, or other plant medicine is what Shamans have done forever to expand their minds and give them an experience of a super-human consciousness.

These are master plants and may be helpful to you on your journey at some point. They will change the way you view the world, which is why many people fear them. Remember what I said about fear.

It is not possible to overdose and die on natural plant medicine, but this is not true for pharmaceuticals.

Learn to not depend on anything, for then it becomes an addiction.

Learn to respect these tools and they will be a source of inspiration, self growth, and self mastery.

Luckily, plant medicines are not nearly as addictive as man made street drugs. They are quite easy to drop if you are mentally strong.

In small doses, they often enhance health, despite what you've learned in health class.

They are often the source of tremendous shamanic power for you as well. This is something few humans know about, yet I suspect the trend will change for we are entering the age of rapid consciousness expansion.

Every shaman will tell you not to abuse plant medicines, not to depend on them, and not to use them regularly.

The following category of drugs must be avoided, for they are highly addictive, expensive and will ruin your life.

They are the ones that man has made.

Cocaine, heroine, crack, these toxic drugs will feel incredible, and are so addictive they will steal your soul, make you poor, ruin your relationships and ruin your life.

So why do people take drugs like this, or use plant medicines recreationally?

In my opinion, it's an escape from dealing with their emotional trauma.

We all have traumas.

Traumas can resurface when you least expect them, and they often feel like tremendous unexplainable emotion or very toxic thoughts or pain in the body that grows and doesn't leave.

The drugs fix that by temporarily taking away the pain and bringing in bliss, which is obviously not sustainable or healthy.

Know that you can become addicted to anything, not just drugs.

Notice what your addictions are. We all have them.

Is it playing video games, is it watching YouTube, is it eating gummies? An addiction is something you do often and you don't know why you're doing it.

A Shaman would call all of these poisons if they are addictive.

Always master them, always delay and defer them, then enjoy them on purpose. For that is totally fine. G-d is in all things, and to deny anything is to deny G-d.

If you choose to try drugs, it's wise to use them on purpose, with intention and in moderation. Know that you can always come to me if you're curious, for I am experienced in these matters.

Similarly, it's best to enjoy your video games, your treats on purpose, with your full attention on them.

Not to do them mindlessly, for that is only an escape from the present moment - the place where life unfolds.

Do not let an unconscious, unhealthy habit form if you can

CHAPTER 10

Money and Material Objects

Money doesn't buy happiness nor does it create health, though it is kingly to have lots of it! It is perfectly fine to want lots of it and to manifest lots of it.

Realize that many people with money are also miserable and sick because they have many fears and they think their money will help with that.

The wise know that you can't take any physical treasure with you when you die.

Thus, the real treasure in life is not money.

Money is energy and it always comes when you need it, for we are always provided for.

Always remember that receiving money is a blessing. Being grateful and appreciating your wealth is truly wise because it attracts more of it to you.

Your material comforts could vanish in a moment, and they are unnecessary for a true man.

A true man can be happy, strong, wise and of service without money, for he knows his time will come again.

Realize that earning money only brings temporary satisfaction.

Also realize that earning money while doing something you don't like doing is empty. Doing that over a long period of time creates mental suffering and stress, which leads to sickness.

Similarly, buying things you want will also only bring temporary happiness. Your tastes will soon change.

Therefore, seek to Know what you truly desire.

Knowledge of your desires along with gratitude allows you to truly create and attract whatever reality you want.

Discover what you truly love.

Discover your talents.

You can become anything, have anything.

Patience and will to focus on your desires are the true treasures.

Therefore, seek employment (or create a business) where you serve others who appreciate what you offer.

The money that arrives from grateful people in need is immensely satisfying, creates health, and attracts more of what you desire.

Your service will feed the trinity of your mind, body, and soul.

Remember, no amount of money will make you safe or happy on a permanent basis.

Knowledge of who you truly are, an eternal spirit here on this planet to learn and evolve, is the inner treasure few have discovered.

CHAPTER 11

Knowledge

Time is not real to those with eternal knowledge.

G-d is the overlord consciousness of ALL things.

All knowledge of all things in the Universe is buried within human DNA. We are the ultimate species!

Remind yourself every day that your soul, your mind, your consciousness (call it what you want), lives forever. It lives on well after the body.

When any soul takes on a body form on earth, (an animal or a human), they have agreed to forget who they were as a soul.

This is the essential part of the schooling of earth.

In this way you can then remember who you were. Oh, that is delightful and divine.

Few realize that death is actually peaceful and pleasurable because they fear it immensely. Many have died consciously and chosen their next bodies.

When this moment is nearing, just breathe. Breathe and release your fears and let the chemicals in your body change your consciousness.

You will feel G-d in these moments.

CHAPTER 12

Earth

Every soul that takes on a human body agrees to forget everything they've ever known in order to come here and learn.

Earth has a heart, a brain and a much bigger soul than anything on the planet including humans.

She's feminine.

Many confuse her as G-d.

She is the daughter of G-d like you are the son.

Earth is known as the Blue Jewel, and she's a unique and special planet.

Her spirit name is known as Gaia.

Earth was seeded by extraterrestrials from the constellation Pleiades.

Pleiadians are super humans with G-dly power.

They are humans, but billions of years into the future.

They are the Greek/Roman 'g-ds' and inhabited earth at one point.

Earth is a free-will zone. This is rare in the Universe. It means you can do anything you want and there is no judgement from G-d. Anything is allowed.

G-d doesn't interfere with human choices in a free-will zone.

G-d desires we find him on our own, oh how satisfying that would be if you were g-d.

Your soul is a drop of the soup of g-d. Seek to remember.

Doing what you can to make Gaia beautiful and showing her inhabitants respect is divinely noble.

CHAPTER 13

G-d

There is a creator.

To be Jewish means to believe in a single Creator.

Though this does not deny the fact that there are other higher beings like angels and other evolved species on other planets with powers far greater than ours.

Your soul contains a slice of Hashem.

G-d is within all things, even the worst things.

To deny anything is to deny G-d.

One of your earthly purposes is to discover the creator yourself.

Everything will be empty, even true love, compared to this.

Seek this treasure my boy, that's where the real gold is.

It is in your heart. Love will guide you there.

CHAPTER 14

Law

When I met G-d my first time, he said to me I can do whatever I want.

He called me his son, as are all humans, and he demanded that I enjoy this realm. This is in the Torah as well.

Though he said I could do whatever I want, there was a catch.

I have to do it with respect and kindness.

Realize that we are here on earth to enjoy, yet as a Jew, we are instructed to act with love and wisdom.

Early Jewish civilizations were tasked with creating the law.

For without the law there is chaos.

But man is flawed, so some of the laws created by humans do not always feel right to a true man to be followed.

For example, what's more important to spend your last dollar on. Paying taxes, or feeding your family?

A true man follows his heart and accepts the consequences of the law with grace.

Do not repeat this to others, keep it to yourself.

Follow your heart and do what feels right.

Do what you want, do it respectfully.

If it scares you, do it scared.

Follow this wisdom and your life will be spectacular.

Seek to learn G-d's laws and master the laws of the Universe.

Obey these laws and your life will be magical.

That's also your purpose.

CHAPTER 15

The Law of One

Everything in the Universe comes from the ONE true creator and is in a constant state of infinite expansion.

I Am is his name.

How can all things contain the One?

Contemplate that often.

Learn to see the Divine in all things and you will become Divine.

Attempt to see how this is in times of conflict and your actions will be curiously different than if not.

Mysteries will be revealed, and assistance will be provided to you from the angels and invisible helpers as you earn trust from the higher realms.

To deny seeing G-d in anything is like denying G-d.

Therefore, there is no good or evil.

There is only Love from this perspective, and it is the highest perspective you can attain.

CHAPTER 16

The Law of Karma

The Law of Karma states that all things have a cause, and all causes create an effect.

This is true for all events going forward and backward to infinity.

Seek to see the causes and effects of everything that happens to you and those around you.

The truth of the matter will keep your mind pure and clean, free from anger and poisoned thoughts.

You will have peace, strength and health.

Your mind and emotions will have equanimity.

Be cautious and discrete in your choices if they are bold, because if you fail to follow man's law, there may be consequences that you will have to be responsible for.

Then again, there may not be if you do not get caught and if your actions are righteous and from the heart.

Failure to follow your heart creates sickness and stress.

Trusting your heart, and acting with wisdom allows you to fly through life as if with wings.

Your life will be magical.

Failure to follow G-d's laws, however, always results in the golden lesson, which becomes increasingly painful until you learn it.

You will receive a consequence in order to learn what you're not seeing.

This is how the soul learns lessons. All the lessons pertain to love and wisdom.

Learning lessons is why you're on earth.

Once your lessons are learned and integrated, you will live a G-dly life on earth.

You will manifest anything you want.

Many go their whole lives not knowing who they are or what they're doing wrong.

They have to come back to earth over and over.

This is the Karma of past lives.

There is much more out there my boy.

CHAPTER 17

The Law of Attraction

The law of Attraction says that there is no repulsion.

There is only attraction. That means you are always attracting things to you even when you're not trying to or thinking about it.

Your beliefs, your thoughts, your emotions are what generates the attraction. G-d, or the Universe is what fulfills the attraction. We are all One, so G-d seeks to make this happen.

This is never not happening, so better pay attention.

For example, sad and angry people attract things that make them more sad or more angry.

Funny thoughts attract humorous situations.

Feeling blessed attracts wealth and blessings.

Feeling love attracts love.

Feeling anger attracts things that make you angry.

Learn to see when you're low, become a master of your mind so you can pivot swiftly.

Always do what feels right and keep your inner peace.

And So It Is

Just as humans were seeded by Pleidians, Pleidians were seeded by the Arcturians.

The Arcturians, billions of years before, were seeded by the Sirians.

This trend will continue, as earth seeds a new planet and plays the role of 'creator'.

One day we will seed a new planet. We are already thinking about doing this on Mars.

This truth of "as above, so below" extends up and down.

There are always worlds contained within worlds.

Below us is the animal world.

Below that there is the insect world.

Below that is the minerals, and the elementals.

This extends into infinity in both directions.

G-d's consciousness is within all of these dimensions.

There is always something bigger and something smaller in life.

Ants in the sand have no knowledge of higher worlds, yet we do of theirs.

Work diligently at your discovered purpose, stay true to that, and trust that all the worlds above will look after you.

As you develop your knowledge of the earth, its creatures, the minutiae of life, it is your duty to safeguard them.

Similarly, always trust that your spiritual parents, your multi-dimensional ancestors, your angels and spirit guides are always watching over you.

They are the ones speaking to your intuition and your gut, for they dwell in the soup that is G-d energy.

Time goes on forever my boy.

We take on many forms.

In this form I am your Dad.

What should we be in our next lifetime?

I love you forever.

Jesse Sternberg is a mindfulness teacher, meditation instructor, and master dog trainer. The founder of the Peaceful Alpha Project, he has been working with animals for more than 30 years, and coaching teens for over 20. Jesse lives in Toronto, Canada.

If this book resonated with you and you'd like to book a free 15-minute coaching session or video chat with me, just email me - jesse@peacefulalpha.com